19 Keys to U

H..

T.R.A.N.S.F.O.R.M.A.T.I.O.N.

Induce Awareness to Enhance Learning Skills by Overcoming Struggles to Infuse Positivity For Exponential Growth in Your Life.

B.R.AMRITAANSHU SAROJ

https://awareonc.com/

https://ahealthybliss.com/

Table of Contents

Introduction

"Competency"

"By stretching yourself beyond your perceived level of confidence you accelerate your development of competence."
- Michael J. Gelb

The reader of this book is currently in either of the following stages of learning:

Stage:1- Unconscious Incompetence

"I don't know that I don't know".
This stage is before reading this book.

Great! Congratulations! You already took action and now you are starting your journey to move one step ahead to reach the next stage.

Stage: 2- Conscious Incompetence

"I know that I don't know".
I want to improve.

Dear lovely readers,
After reading this book, you gain the concept knowledge to work on your mindset and be an action taker.

Thereafter, your next step to reach the stage is conscious competence. The next book in the series on various activities is about this next stage.

Stage:3- Conscious competence

I know that I know.

"I know how to do it but I have to concentrate on my task".

In this stage you start building your skill as per your current capability and keep on practicing for attainment of higher laurels.

From here you need to start practicing and applying your learning in your daily routine.

Stage: 4- Unconscious competence

"I can do it with ease and habitually".

You have enhanced your capability, better personal growth and skill development. You have practiced so much that you are in a flow state of mind. You can do your tasks with ease, unconsciously.

You are now in the Natural default set of Happy Transformation.

Want to know what's 5th stage is?

Well, you will know and understand if you take notes and stay aware taking key lessons to implement the processes mentioned, while reading this book till the end. Happy Transformation is a journey as positive intention brings positive results.

Intention of writing this book is to bring a positive impact to the reader's life.

This book emphasizes on readers' happiness as well as aspires to **inspire, illuminate, touch, and enlighten readers through its presence.**

Even if it brings about positive impact on any reader, it does make a difference!
It's worth taking action for writing a book that brings about positive impact. I believe that this book will do the same.

Always be grateful for what you have and what you can give!

The realization that your life can be helpful and can inspire other people, brings about an unadulterated feeling of liberty and bliss.

"Happiness lies in the joy of achievement and the thrill of creative effort." —Franklin D. Roosevelt

"Be kind whenever possible. It is always possible." —The Dalai Lama

Acronym
H.A.P.P.Y. T.R.A.N.S.F.O.R.M.A.T.I.O.N.
originates from the following idea.

Every human on planet earth has certain kinds of **needs**. We live in the **social network of an ecosystem**. We survive and thrive by being part of an environment. We are happy and satisfied when our needs get fulfilled. This is the very mainspring of whatever we do and whatever we put up with and which is: all of us want to be happy and satisfied.

You are **aware** of the **reason** for that particular need. You have a **purpose** to fulfill it. For example, food as a physiological need. You need food to survive and thrive. Your **brain** and body functions depend on it. You also need rest and **adequate sleep** for the brain and body to work properly.

Therefore, you need to take **action** to earn for the food you eat. **Personal** and **technical** skills and **development** act as a catalyst to enable you to earn your bread. You need to **focus** to certain traits to learn, earn and grow. You also need to keep yourself **motivated** till the end in order to fulfill your needs.

You also can create or grasp the **opportunities** meet your requirements through dedicated effort. Everyone's journey of life is full of challenges and experiences. You keep on modifying your learnings or **conditioning** of mind for better responses to these events, challenges and experiences. There will be few ups and downs and you must know how to be **resilient** in order to overcome all resistances. How you deal with your life's challenges when they confront you, emphasizes your **level of consciousness**. You become more **intuitive** in nature through every lesson that you receive from each experience. You become a lifelong learner from your life journey and experiences that propel you towards a higher scale of consciousness which in turn inspires you to **open your heart for noble causes**.

Always be grateful for what you have and what you can give.

It's not happiness that makes us grateful. It's gratefulness that makes us happy.

Gratitude and appreciation comes from within through attainment of higher consciousness. These verities cannot be taught of implanted; they have to be recognized, expressed, inculcated, cultivated and propagated.

Gratitude for even tiny aspects brings about happiness and positivity.

The visualization of the various principles in the book aims to bring about positivity and happiness through simple manifestations of mind, behaviour and belief.

"Show Gratitude"

As

"Positive Intentions Bring Positive Results"

"Happiness cannot be traveled to owned, earned, worn or consumed. Happiness is the spiritual experience of living every minute with love, grace, and gratitude."

- Denis Waitley

H.A.P.P.Y.
T.R.A.N.S.F.O.R.M.A.T.I.O.N.

(: Higher levels of Consciousness :)

"If you want to find the secrets of the universe, think in terms of energy, frequency, and vibration."
- Nikola Tesla

The environment is full of different energies, frequencies, and vibrations. The body vibrates at a certain frequency that varies as per external and internal stimulus. The energies which are quite alike electrical and magnetic fields stimulate chemical processes in the body influencing health and behavioral patterns. To recognize the positive and attain the energetic vibrations generated within and around the body requires elevating one's thought processes to a higher level to obtain a pragmatic impact. One needs to garner self-awareness to visualize how thoughts and behavior affect the rhythms of the body. One needs to move towards a higher consciousness of creative energy.

The moment one accepts one's entity and not indulges in self- denial, the person is propelled towards self-improvement. That very moment one starts attracting growth and prosperity in life. One must be a lifelong learner. It is necessary to keep on learning something new and implementing the same in the daily routine and spread the lessons far and wide. This golden triangle principle transforms one's life as well as others to create a ripple effect.

Negative thinking drains your energy and exhausts you to be unkind to yourself in your mind and with everybody you meet. Higher levels of consciousness help you to regain your energy and attain love, peace and joy. Your vital energy helps you to be kind and generous.

You can unlock higher levels of consciousness by stopping to overthink. Overthinking blocks the mind from going beyond itself. You start your journey by acceptance and being aware of a high level of consciousness and allowing self-talk. When you ask the magic questions to yourself, you manage to look beyond the mind and not at the mind. You arise from the recesses of mediocrity of thought process to attain self-realization. Self realization enlightens you to understand what truly matters - love, peace and joy towards ultimate pure consciousness. These are three aspects of the deep states of inner connectedness with being.

Enlightened consciousness or pure consciousness is free from the tangible attachments of the physical and mental forms. The moment you come into the mode of acceptance, you get free from the dominance of the mind and revert to your complete acceptance of what reconnects you with your complete self. This leads to the end of all misconceptions and pre-conceived notions of your life. A fully conscious person doesn't get involved in arguments, no matter how hard the other person tries. A higher state of consciousness can help you to see the cause of the problem and attain a higher echelon of thought process.

In the States of West Bengal and some North Eastern and Eastern states of India, the Goddess *Kali* is worshipped with all pomp, gaiety and deep devotion. However, even the staunchest devotee of the present times will struggle to explain the word *Kali* to its true virtue. To a layman *"Kali"* resembles the dark complexion of the Goddess.
However, the truth is astounding. Kali is an acronym of the words Kaal (time) and Ether (space). This had been once postulated by

Albert Einstein as the 4th and 5th dimensions of energy and matter. Those who can surpass the transcendental state of time and space like *Ramakrishna Paramhansa* are known to attain the KALI consciousness.

Your thoughts are your life experiences. Your thoughts try to make sense of everything for your survival. You become aware by listening to your thoughts. Your awareness helps to differentiate between the thoughts that propel you forward with the ones that hold you back. Higher consciousness is found by talking less, listening more, and being aware of the environment within every discussion. Awareness is the key for you to move towards a higher level of consciousness. This helps you to find an empowering meaning in your life.

The method of dealing with challenges in life reveals the level of your consciousness. Higher states of consciousness can help you unlock the next level and can amplify your own ability to experience it. To accelerate, you must surround yourself with those people who want to achieve the same. Remember that a positive environment always invites positivity in the form of peace, love, happiness, respect, gratitude, appreciation etc.

You are born to do incredible things in your life. It all starts with your intention towards your process to achieve whatever you aim for. Fruitful results happen through your own higher level of consciousness which gives you satisfaction, fulfillment and a path to follow. The sense of fulfillment comes by raising your vibrations for attaining creative energy. For example, ripple effect - the real story of a mom and her 3 year old kid bringing positive impact to the lives of many and another real story of a doctor dad and his daughter in the first chapter of my previous book Happy Transformation.

H.**A**.P.P.Y.
T.R.A.N.S.F.O.R.M.A.T.I.O.N.

(: Awareness :)

"Awareness is like the Sun. When it shines on the things, they're transformed."
- Thich Nhat Hanh

If you had the choice, would you rather be smarter than you are or more aware?

The argument for being more aware is rarely made, yet by far choosing to be more aware is the better choice — and unlike IQ, you can increase your awareness.

Being smart, even very, very smart, doesn't immunize you from living unconsciously. An unconscious life is driven by habits, fixed beliefs, second-hand opinions, social pressure, peer-group values, and old conditioning. To realize this, and then to escape its grip, requires awareness, not IQ.

Awareness brings freedom from fixed beliefs and habits. You are the awareness from which everything is made. It is a psychological state that is central to which you are considering different aspects including feelings, traits, and behaviour. It emerges at different moments according to the circumstances.

Research suggests awareness can make you more proactive, boost your acceptance, and encourage positive self-development. Self-awareness allows you to see things from the perspective of others. You get better in practicing self-control, work creatively and productively. Your self-esteem gets elevated and you experience pride in yourself and your work. It leads to better decision making. It can make you better in your communication at your workplace or at home. Your self-confidence and job-related wellbeing is enhanced and you stand out of the crowd.

Being aware aligns you with the creative impulse in nature. Awareness helps in developing empathy, understanding differences between people, and to value diversity. You become aware of your strengths and weaknesses. This enhances your confidence to work on it and be open-minded. Therefore, you are less judgmental and aware of your own characteristics.

You are enlightened and feel a shift from inside once you gain insights. You explore and understand what things matter to you and find them valuable. Your radical shift from inside intensifies the qualities of awareness. The essential qualities that matter for being human include personal evolution, curiosity, creativity, love and compassion. These valued qualities are the source to evolve as a proper human being. Awareness brings you close to this wonder. Everything you value and do comes from inside. Let your awareness guide you to your goal - applying ideas to plan and execute.

Awareness often leads to application if the threads are seriously and meticulously followed. Everyone sees an apple or any other object fall but it was Newton who had thought about gravity from this seemingly commonplace occurrence. The birds in the sky prompted the Wright Brothers to make an effort to emulate them. Steam from the kettle had directed James Watt towards the idea of a steam engine. Thus, awareness is a verity that can grow a form of curiosity even with the mundane and bring about evolutionary discoveries.

Mollah Naseeruddin had promised to himself that he would never tell a lie. Every morning he used to pack his donkeys with sacks of old clothes to wash them by the river outside town. On his way, he always crossed a police check post where a constable would ask him the same two questions – "Who are you?" and "What do you do?"

Naseeruddin would also reply with the same answers "I am Naseeruddin" and "I am a thief".

Hearing this, the constable would check all his sacks and his clothes to discover the loot, if any but never could he recover anything other than old, dirty and torn clothes.

This continued for 20 years until finally one day the constable had to retire from his services.

One day, the constable saw Mollah Naseeruddin at the marketplace. He ran up to him and said in a panting plea, "See, now I am retired. I can do no harm to you. For twenty years you have been telling me that you were a thief but we could not recover anything from you. Kindly tell me now what the things that you stole are?"

Naseeruddin smiled in mute glee and finally said."Brother, I had been stealing donkeys."

H.A.**P**.P.Y.
T.R.A.N.S.F.O.R.M.A.T.I.O.N.

(: Purpose :)

"Nobody ever wrote down a plan to be broke, fat, lazy or stupid. Those things are what happen when you don't have a plan."
- Larry Winget

Plan how you will spend your time and what you will prioritize.

You seek meaning and direction in your life. You are able to identify the things that matter to you. Your sense of purpose is shaped by things that you believe in and value for. Your purpose to pursue it gives satisfaction in your life. You feel good with the way your actions bring about a sense of meaning to you. Everything good or bad in your life is meant to uncover your purpose. Your circumstances, challenges and experiences shift your viewpoint.

You start awakening your purpose once you start believing in your capacity to change the world. Your purpose is aligned with your mind, body and soul for greater sense, cause and effect. Your purpose makes you aware how you can contribute to the world. You understand the value of your environment and ecosystem. Your better sense of purpose motivates you to bring profound positive impact to your family members, friends, community and the world thereby creating a positive ripple effect.

Studies at various levels show that people with a clear sense of purpose are more likely to grow old in a healthy way as they find it easier to be inspired by the things they do.

Your sense of purpose gives you better vision. You can become crystal clear about how to achieve and proceed for bigger long-term goals with the help of smaller short-term goals. You can become proactive to prioritize your life, make better plans and become efficient in executing those plans. You can understand, respect and value all kinds of relations. You can get better in identifying the things that truly count if circumstances change. You can become more resilient as you grow and keep on going to fulfill your purpose. You can accomplish your purpose with positive energy and motivation. This is one of the fundamental factors of happiness, health and longevity.

All of this can happen only if you have a proper plan and purpose before you. A goal is a plan with a timeline. A goal should also have a meaningful purpose and the best way to achieve a goal is not to get overwhelmed with it. Break the ultimate goal into yearly , monthly, weekly, daily even hourly fragments to achieve fulfillment as you go ahead. Self appreciation is the best gift one can present oneself with.

You must always have a purpose-driven life. Make purpose a tool to transform into a better, happier, and healthier life. You must first transform yourself in order to transform others' lives and create abundance in the ecosystem. For example, the inspiring and touching real story of Jacqueline Way and Nic Way in my previous book Happy Transformation. This lovely story of a mom and her 3 year old kid teaches us so many lessons and inspires us to be a giver. How their purpose of 365 give back something to the world - people, animals and our planet creates a ripple effect of happiness all around the world and brings positive impact to the lives of many.

Happiness can come from queer plans. We provide our minds with affirmations to bring a sense of happiness of fulfillment of a task.

Here's a queer example:

A man observed a woman in the grocery store with a three year old girl in her basket. As they passed the cookie section, the little girl asked for cookies and her mother told her no. The little girl immediately began to whine and fuss, and the mother said quietly, "Now Monica, we just have half of the aisles left to go through; don't be upset. It won't be long."

Soon they came to the candy aisle, and the little girl began to shout for candy. And when told she couldn't have any, began to cry. The mother said, "There, there, Monica, don't cry–only two more aisles to go, and then we'll be checking out."

When they got to the check-out stand, the little girls immediately began to clamor for gum and burst into a terrible tantrum upon discovering there'd be no gum purchased. The mother patiently said, "Monica, we'll be through this checkout stand in 5 minutes and then you can go home and have a nice nap."

The man followed them out to the parking lot and stopped the woman to compliment her. "I couldn't help noticing how patient you were with little Monica," he began. Whereupon the mother said, "I'm Monica . . . my little girl's name is Tammy."

Imagine you had a bank account that deposited $86,400 each morning. The account carries over no balance from day to day, allows you to keep no cash balance, and every evening cancels whatever part of the amount you had failed to use during the day. What would you do? Draw out every dollar each day!

We all have such a bank. Its name is Time. Every morning, it credits you with 86,400 seconds. Every night it writes off, as lost, whatever time you have failed to use wisely. It carries over no balance from day to day. It allows no overdraft so you can't borrow against yourself or use more time than you have. Each day, the account starts fresh. Each night, it destroys an unused time. If you fail to use the day's deposits, it's your loss and you can't appeal to get it back.

There is never any borrowing time. You can't take a loan out on your time or against someone else's. The time you have is the time you have and that is that. Time management is yours to decide how you spend the time, just as with money you decide how you spend the money. It is never the case of us not having enough time to do things, but the case of whether we want to do them and where they fall in our priorities.

H.A.P.**P**.Y.
T.R.A.N.S.F.O.R.M.A.T.I.O.N.

(: Personal Development :)

"Personal development is the belief that you are worth the effort, time, and energy needed to develop yourself."
- Denis Waitley

Personal development is a lifelong process to build your potential to make you a better version of yourself. It develops your capabilities through various activities and enhances your personality. For example, an educational program mentioned in my previous book Happy Transformation talks about a tool for teachers that integrate a simple daily giving practice with their curriculum and they called it the 365 give challenge. It's unique because it's powered by kids. They choose how they are going to give, support causes, and impact the world in ways that they innovate.

It is a transformational pathway to your satisfaction and success in your life. For this you need to embrace certain self-improvement skills.

There are a few traits which you already possess naturally and a few are gained through education and training. This improves your learning preferably under the guidance from a mentor to overcome challenges and have better understanding from your past mistakes to avoid them in the future. Your level of self-awareness grows better if you start acknowledging your shortcomings. Once you start seeing the bigger picture, holding yourself accountable for your mistakes and working on solutions to improve yourself, self transformation will bound to happen which in turn will bring in fulfillment.

You need to constantly strive for improvement for brain efficiency and flourish. You must keep on learning and implementing the same to enhance your personal growth. You need to be proactive and take charge of your actions to up skill your level to achieve your goals.

Personal development gives you clarity by helping you define your personal vision and all the goals you wish to accomplish in your life. When you have clarity, you work better in strategizing the various plans and how to execute those on the basis of your objectives.

Personal development helps you to discover your hidden potential by utilizing your knowledge, more and more by working on your abilities and enhancing your skills. You become more confident in coming out of your comfort zone, pushing your boundaries, and exploring new things. Personal development empowers you to take control of things and motivates you for constant improvement. You are satisfied with your performance and increase in your productivity.

Obstacles should not deter you because they are part of life.

There once was a very wealthy and curious king. This king had a huge boulder placed in the middle of a road. Then he hid nearby to see if anyone would try to remove the gigantic rock from the road.

The first people to pass by were some of the king's wealthiest merchants and courtiers. Rather than moving it, they simply walked around it. A few loudly blamed the King for not maintaining the roads. Not one of them tried to move the boulder.

Finally, a peasant came along. His arms were full of vegetables. When he got near the boulder, rather than simply walking around it as the others had, the peasant put down his load and tried to move the stone to the side of the road. It took a lot of effort but he finally succeeded.

The peasant gathered up his load and was ready to go on his way when he saw a purse lying in the road where the boulder had been. The peasant opened the purse. The purse was stuffed full of gold coins and a note from the king. The king's note said the purse's gold was a reward for moving the boulder from the road.

The king showed the peasant what many of us never understand: every obstacle presents an opportunity to improve our condition.

A man's favorite donkey falls into a deep precipice. He can't pull it out no matter how hard he tries. He therefore decides to bury it alive.
Soil is poured onto the donkey from above. The donkey feels the load, shakes it off, and steps on it. More soil is poured.

It shakes it off and steps up. The more the load was poured, the higher it rose. By noon, the donkey was grazing in green pastures.

After much shaking off (of problems) And stepping up (learning from them), One will graze in GREEN PASTURES.

"Out of clutter, find simplicity. From discord, find harmony. In the middle of difficulty lies opportunity."

— Albert Einstein

H.A.P.P.Y.
T.R.A.N.S.F.O.R.M.A.T.I.O.N.

(: You :)

"The only person you are destined to become is the person you decide to be."
- Ralph Waldo Emerson

Do you have those days where you feel down in the dumps?

When everything seems to go wrong and before you know it, you are starting to tell yourself you are no good?

Have you ever considered all of the gifts you uniquely bring to the world?

You have special gifts or skills that you share each and every day that positively affect the people in your life.

There are a few situations when you have self-doubt. There are certain moments of your life when you feel like you are not good enough for anyone. Sometimes a few challenges come your way that questions your self-worth. You might feel low in confidence and self-esteem due to many ups and downs in your life. Everyone faces ups and downs in their life. So you are not alone to experience that in your life journey.

The strongest words are those words which you say to yourself. Those words can either make you or break you. The words which you say to others also affect you first because you are the first person who hears those words. Therefore, choose your words wisely and carefully because like everybody else your life and words matter for the propagation of mankind.

The words that you think or speak are full of energy, vibration, and frequency. If you use words which are of the nature of negative and destructive energy then you are vibrating at low frequency and vice-versa. You must decide what kind of energy you want to transfer to yourself as well as to others. That's how the transformation of your life depends.

We all have a few similarities but go through overall different life journeys. Everyone has their real stories to share about how they have overcome their struggles. They need to inspire others who might be going through the same hurdles/ challenges.

You matter because you are unique like your fingerprints. You are the only person who has a unique and unheralded story to tell because of your challenges and experiences. You have different abilities and talents. You are talented enough to inspire someone seeking for help out there. It's your moral responsibility to share with the world your learnings and lessons of life. It's now your turn to bring a positive impact on others' lives. Yes! You have a message to share with the whole world. You can influence and make that someone realize their uniqueness and the possibility to achieve their greatness. Therefore, you act as a catalyst to make a difference in the lives of others. You have this capability to put a smile on someone's face, all you need is little acts of random kindness.

Even if you bring a positive impact on one, it's worth sharing your message. Your message must be natural and authentic. Your message is valuable to many who resonate with your message and you. Over the period of time, it definitely creates positive ripple effects for many.

You can consciously be in the state of the embodiment of love, peace, joy from your outside environment only and only when you are in the same state from inside. This is because 75% of your state is the inside environment i.e. emotional, mental, spiritual, and only 25% is your outside environment i.e. physical. So, you need to stop blaming the circumstances and go for self-improvement. 80% of those circumstances are created by your own inside environment and only 20% are by your outside environment.

- From my previous book (:Happy Transformation :)

What kind of footprint do you want to leave behind?

You are that human being that has useful space on earth to make a difference by being active, breathing and living for sharing your message. You are here to accomplish everything you need to and light up the world with your presence. Be positive, be happy, and most importantly, be yourself, because you are important in every aspect of your own. You have come to inspire, illuminate, touch, and enlighten others through your presence.

H.A.P.P.Y.
T.R.A.N.S.F.O.R.M.A.T.I.O.N.

(: Technical development :)

"You never change things by fighting the existing reality. To change something, build a new model that makes the existing model obsolete."
- Buckminster Fuller

It's an age of digital revolution and learning technology skills is crucial for you to have a development mindset and improve your learning agility.

Even an Engineering giant like L&T uses the slogan of 3Ts : Training, Technology and Timeliness.

Technology is gradually infiltrating every part of our work and it's likely to continue to do so in the future. It has improved access to information in an exponential way. It has revolutionized our work processes and has enriched our lives with greater convenience.
For example, MRI scanner - Magnetic resonance imaging is a medical imaging technique used in radiology to form pictures of the anatomy and the physiological

processes of the body. The people who donate for various charitable causes, bear semblances of happiness inside them. When you look at the functional MRIs of these people, scientists have found that the act of giving stimulates the *Mesolimbic* pathway, which is the reward center in the brain. The brain releases Endorphins and creates what is known as the "helper's high."

It is helping to automate manual tasks, so processes run more efficiently and enables us to make innovative and intelligent decisions faster to produce quality goods and services. It eases the use of economic resources by encompassing a huge body of knowledge and tools. The upgraded and advanced technology is important for economic growth and development of both local and global markets. It saves time, increases employment and has a huge effect on ability and efficiency on business's output rate leading to higher profit and greater economic development.

Technical skills are increasingly important for everyone, regardless of industry or job role. Every industry relies on advanced technology. You become ready and adaptable by developing your technical skills and add value to your future-proof career.

You feel more comfortable and become confident by understanding, learning and implementing the technology better. Thus, your work efficiency and effectiveness gets enriched and enhanced.

You flourish in your life with the proper understanding of technology usage. Knowledge is a potential power to transform your life into a better version. You must focus on continuous learning of upgrading technology to become smarter and stand out from the crowd. Your work becomes more productive with the use of technology and motivates you to achieve higher goals.

"Let's go invent tomorrow instead of worrying about what happened yesterday."
– Steve Jobs

"Once a new technology rolls over you, if you're not part of the steamroller, you're part of the road."
– Stewart Brand

H.A.P.P.Y.
T.**R**.A.N.S.F.O.R.M.A.T.I.O.N.

(: Resilience :)

"There is nothing good or bad but thinking makes it so."
- William Shakespeare, Hamlet

Have you ever wondered why some people remain calm in the face of adversity, while others crumble?

Psychologists call resilience as an ability to effectively bounce back from adversity.

Whenever you come across a difficult situation, you have two choices:

1- You can either let your emotions get the best of you and become paralyzed by fear.

Or,

2- You can uplift yourself from the negative and transform pain into possibility.

Which one do you want to choose?

You must have the ability to learn how to adapt as per the different kinds of situations you go through. You really need to find ways to bounce back when something difficult happens in your life. For example, the real life story of Sam Botta mentioned in my previous book Happy Transformation who had a terrible car accident, a top radio voiceover artist, who literally lost the ability to speak. The physical movement technique mentioned in that book to program certain neural pathways of the brain helped him to recover better.

You must be aware of how to overcome your obstacles. The first aspect, of course, is the unrelenting "will" to succeed. The second most important aspect is not to get overwhelmed by a problem or failure and remain positive on the face of adversity.

"I have not failed. I've just found 10,000 ways that won't work."
– Thomas Edison

Resilience enables you to have an ability to overcome overwhelming experiences that might lead to emotional or mental health issues. It develops mechanisms to protect and create balance in your life when a difficult situation comes about.

Your learning capability gets impacted through your positivity which leads to better academic performances and improvement in other aspects of life - personal and professional. It helps in reducing the risk taking behaviours like drinking, smoking or use of drugs. You become more social and increase your involvement in various activities - family or community. Being resilient and beating your resistance makes you better and stronger on all health levels - emotional, mental, physical and spiritual taking social and economic factors into account as well. Therefore, the mortality rate gets reasonably lowered.

Your lifestyle and daily routine is a vital factor to beat your resistances and become more resilient. You must bring necessary changes in your life and learn to adapt as per the situation. Your thoughts that drive your emotions determine your resilience. You must not automatically assume that everything happened was your fault or somebody else's fault. You must not jump into some random conclusions. You must pause for a moment when you get an emotional reaction. Then you must try and tune into what that interpretation is that you are making about what had happened.

Checking that interpretation accuracy is the first step of having more resilient mindset.

Your life journey is full of challenges and experiences. These experiences may bend you, but they do not have to break you. There will be few ups and downs and you must know how to cope up and be aware how to develop strategies that make you better resilient. You are resilient enough if you are able to effectively navigate the highs and lows of your life. Thus, you become more confident in your abilities to tackle all kinds of situations. You must be a lifelong learner as your life is a journey. Your journey towards a higher level of consciousness makes you resilient.

"When we learn how to become resilient, we learn how to embrace the beautifully broad spectrum of the human experience."
- Jaeda Dewalt

H.A.P.P.Y.
T.R.A.N.S.F.O.R.M.A.T.I.O.N.

(: Action :)

"Do you want to know who you are? Don't ask. Act! Action will delineate and define you."

- Thomas Jefferson

Are you an action taker?

We don't always do as other people tell us to do, we rather do as other people do and this is important when it comes to creating well-being in ourselves and in others.

Just knowing is not sufficient. Awareness is important. Thinking over anything is not adequate, taking action is important. Mind wandering, procrastination, over thinking, analysis paralysis is part of life but it's not worth to resist and limit yourself in a virtual cage. You must come out of this psychological captivity by taking action. You must overcome virtual reality too by being consciously aware of what is happening around you that affects you from inside.

Have you ever found yourself in a situation where you really had been worried about something and you kept worrying even though you knew that worrying wouldn't change the situation? Nevertheless, all you could do was worry and that was the only thing you had done.

According to a study by Daniel Gilbert and Matthew Killingsworth, our mind wanders 46.9 percent of the time we spend awake. Yes, our thoughts are automatic and they have a life of their own. Therefore change will never happen through positive thinking only you have to take positive action too. It's time that we start talking more about how we can take positive action and actually make a change in our lives.

For example,

1- Keep your focus on your breath, don't think about anything else for 5 minutes.

2- Raise hands for 5 minutes.

Which one would be better achievable?

Of course, option 2.

It's really difficult to control our thoughts and we have a better chance at controlling our actions. In our behavior, therefore, well-being is better built by positive action and not only by positive thinking alone.

Taking action helps you to overcome all those low level contracted energies like fear, anxiety, pessimism, skepticism etc. Taking action to try and test something new expands your comfort zone or sometimes helps you to come out of your comfort zone to get benefitted and create a positive outcome. You must take your first step to progress in your life. Taking action for the first step is difficult as you come out of your comfort level but it's worth is immense to propel you towards positive results.

Taking action helps to fulfill your desire to achieve anything you want. You must have a mission, vision, plan the detailed strategy how to move forward and take action. You must consider this as a first baby step towards your ultimate objective. Therefore, focus on a fixed goal but be flexible in the journey to achieve it.

You must consider that it's your responsibility to turn your knowledge into inspired action to others. If inspiration is lost or inspiration is not present then action looks dull. You must take inspired action to serve others with your knowledge and bring a positive impact to the lives of many. This is real success and accomplishments for you. Therefore, making social connections are very important in your life to achieve whatever you want.

It takes **positive action** but some actions are more powerful than others when it comes to **happiness.** Investing your time and heart into the relationships around you, no matter if it's at work or with neighbors or with family or friends this might be one of the most powerful things that you can do for yourself. So, the more you can **turn your thought into action** by being more **understanding and caring** not just towards others but also towards yourself.

"The universe doesn't give you what you ask for with your thoughts; it gives you what you demand with your actions."
- Dr. Steve Maraboli

H.A.P.P.Y.
T.R.A.**N**.S.F.O.R.M.A.T.I.O.N.

(: Network & Ecosystem :)

"Only through our connectedness to others can we really know and enhance the self. And only through working on the self can we begin to enhance our connectedness to others."- Harriet Goldhor Lerner

We live in the social network of an ecosystem. We survive and thrive by being part of an environment that sustains us. Human beings are social creatures and have evolved to live in social groups so whether we are introverts or extroverts, we all need to feel connected to other people. If we don't feel connected and feel lonely for prolonged periods of time, it can actually increase the chances of descending into the pitfalls of depression and augur as bad for our physical health as smoking or obesity.

A great way of feeling connected to people whether close to us or complete strangers is actually thinking about what we can do for "other people."For example, family - fun project and educational program - 365 give challenges mentioned in the book Happy Transformation.

Building networks in different communities is very important. Everything is interconnected. We need to cherish all kinds of relationships. Relationship quality, the positive and negative feelings about a relationship, is an evaluation of the individual's relationship. Relationship quality involves nurturance, affection, intimacy, wellbeing, understanding, validation, care, and even forgivingness.

The National Institute of Health reports that your relationships have a "powerful effect" on your health. If you want to raise your vibe, lower your stress levels, and live a longer, healthier life, it's important to develop a network of relationships. You must share your interests, provide brain-stimulating conversations and imbue your life with a sense of belonging and self-worth.

The prime wealth that one is ever yearning for is health. You must focus on boosting your health. Health must be the center of all concerns. Research says that people who give social support to others have a lower blood pressure. People who interact and support others also help them to recover from coronary-related events. Researchers also say that people who give their time to help others through community and organizational involvement have greater self-esteem, less depression, and lower stress levels. Studies show that giving can actually boost your physical and mental health. Health benefits associated with giving also include longer life, greater happiness, and satisfaction.

- From my previous book (: Happy Transformation :)

"The greatest influence in your life, stronger than your willpower, is your environment. Change that, if necessary. Until you are mentally strong, you can never be what you want to be without a good environment."
- Paramahansa Yogananda

H.A.P.P.Y.
T.R.A.N.S.F.O.R.M.A.T.I.O.N.

(: Self-conditioning :)

"It is your reaction to adversity, not the adversity itself, that determines how your life's story will develop."
— Dieter F. Uchtdorf

Who am I?

Conditioning in behavioral psychology is a theory that the reaction ("response") to an object or event ("stimulus") by a person or animal can be modified by 'learning', or conditioning. Therefore, you can gain control over your reaction or response to an event or stimulus which is not under your control mechanism. Your response, good or bad, as per event will decide the desired outcome or result. So, events will keep on happening but it's your ability to respond to that event that makes you responsible for the outcome.

For example, the current pandemic situation all around the world is a malaise that is testing us, Humans, with our ability to respond for our survival as an outcome. Therefore, it's our responsibility to follow certain rules and regulations to escape extermination of the Human species. This is the ultimate outcome we all want.

Another example is about the real story of Sam Botta mentioned in the Happy Transformation book no.1 of this series.

You must be a lifelong learner because you need to keep on modifying your learnings or conditioning for better responses to unpredictable events. Therefore, your focus must be on self-education. The best investment of time, energy, effort, and money is on self-education. Self-education is the best education which brings about positive impact to self as well as to others, directly and indirectly, thereby creating a positive ripple effect. Researches suggest that the people who are lifelong learners, they are happier, healthier and live longer.

Conditioning is your life changing factor to make you a better person as a whole. Your conditioning determines your concepts in every context. Your self-concept is important because it influences how you feel, think and take action. You are under the influence of your self-concept everyday and everywhere.

The different kinds of interactions with people, social media etc. and their influence develops your self-concept. Understanding the self-concept is important for you because self- knowledge helps you to understand why you do the things you do and how your beliefs and behaviours affect you as well as others around you-for better and for worse. This is one of many factors but powerful influences that help in filtering the perceived information in the environment you live in.

When your concepts are crystal clear, you set up a set of belief systems around yourself. You must make sure that you are not getting trapped in firm beliefs and limiting your beliefs over just a few concepts built by being in a particular environment. Your environment has a great influence over you. In the environment you live in, you must keep on observing, analyzing, evaluating, and verifying again and again over a period of time. That's how your belief system keeps on expanding. You must never limit your beliefs, instead, keep on learning and working towards empowering your beliefs. Your attitude keeps on fluctuating as per your belief system. This induces a certain kind of behaviour pattern in your life as per circumstances you face. Therefore, your particular behaviour as response directs towards a particular result. Thus, self-conditioning plays a vital role in your life which can transform you from rags to riches or vice versa.

Your perceived information as an external stimulus is a factor of your mental conditioning. You must be aware of your present moment through self-observation. You must objectively observe yourself to get in touch with your emotions, feelings, thoughts, actions and bodily sensations. Self-observation helps in conditioning yourself better and which in turn reprograms your mind, body, and soul. Your intention to bring greater awareness into your life helps you to realize your true potential. Give time to yourself and work on your conditioning to have the right mindset to achieve your goals. Your behavior with the right mindset yields positive results.

Look for the ways to work on your limitless potential to be a better version of yourself. It is only limited by your conditioning, concept-context, thinking pattern, belief system, actions, and behavior that are yielding fruitful or futile results. It all starts with your intention towards your process to achieve anything you want.

- From my previous book (: Happy Transformation :)

"True humility is not thinking less of yourself; it is thinking of yourself less."
- Rick Warren

H.A.P.P.Y.
T.R.A.N.S.F.O.R.M.A.T.I.O.N.

(: Focus :)

"The secret of change is to focus all your energy not fighting the old, but building the new." - Dan Millman

"Energy flows where the attention goes". When you focus on something, it expands.

Focus plays an important role in your personal productivity. Focus involves the ability to pay attention to finish things and move one step ahead. Focus helps in optimizing the time for needed work efforts. Focusing on relevant information, analyzing and generating the desired outcome increases productivity.

Focus is the gateway to perception, reasoning, learning and taking decisions. Your ability to respond gets better with good focus. Your capability and effectiveness increases with better focus to finish work.

Focus helps to beat your resistances like procrastination or mind wandering over your quality, efficiency and timeliness. Focus is an essential tool for success. Success is achieved through quality work and the outcome of an effective action taken through dedicated focus on the ultimate goal.

You must declutter your mind to improve focus. You must prioritize your daily tasks and clear your mind of anything that doesn't relate to your prioritized tasks. You must declutter your workspace as well because that also helps you to be more focused. Simplify your workspace by removing unnecessary things which don't relate to your work and only have specific work function related things around you.

Make your workplace clean and inviting for you to work and keep certain things within your reach that bring smiles and happiness to you.

Research has shown that there is no such thing as multitasking when it comes to work. According to the Dent Neurologic Institute, the brain can't multitask. Instead, it switches between tasks which increases errors and makes things take longer. Research has also shown that people who call themselves as multitaskers are in fact worse performers. To focus when it's time to get work done, turn off your distractions- television, social media, phone calls messages, notifications.

When you know what's important in your life and you are determined to reach your goal, the resolve itself makes you feel more positive. You improve your focus and feel more controlled in your life. When you have clarity of what you need to do, you are committed to work with focus to achieve your goal. You must keep consistent on measuring your progress on a day to day basis. You need to be mindful of your plan to follow it. The satisfied experience comes with practice and better choices over the period of time. There will be insecurities and doubts but you need to learn from them and resolve them. You need to understand to transform yourself from learnings and have a firm belief in your capabilities. Your psychological state of being optimistic and in focused determination helps you to be successful in your life.

You must create an environment that allows you to perform your best to finish your task. This can be achieved by going through the process of what you need to do to complete your assigned curriculum. You must be focused in the present moment and let go of the past worries or future speculations. This helps you to bolster your productivity by blocking out the distractions and focusing right now and here in the present moment. Your ability to focus on one thing at a time consistently makes you efficient and effective in your all endeavors.

"When you focus on problems, you'll have more problems. When you focus on possibilities, you'll have more opportunities. Dream, Wish, and Make it happen."
- Quote from allauthor.com

H.A.P.P.Y.
T.R.A.N.S.F.**O**.R.M.A.T.I.O.N.

(: Opportunity :)

"Opportunities are presented to us each and everyday, but do we see them. To see an opportunity we must be open to all thoughts."
- Catherine Pulsifer

Opportunity is the gift within every gift and we have this saying, opportunity knocks only once.

Well, think again.

Every moment is a new gift, over and over again and if you miss the opportunity of this moment, another moment is given to us, and then another.

We can avail ourselves of this opportunity or we can miss it and if we avail ourselves of this opportunity, it is the key to happiness. We behold the master key to our happiness in our own hands. Moment by moment, we can be grateful for this gift.

We can be grateful for every opportunity that comes our way and even when we are confronted with something that is terribly difficult, **we can rise** to the occasion and respond to the opportunity that has been given to us.

"In the middle of a difficulty lies opportunity." - Albert Einstein

It isn't as bad as it might seem. Actually, when you look at it and experience it, you will find that most of the time, what is given to us is the opportunity to enjoy. We only miss it because we are rushing through life and we are not stopping to see the opportunity. However, once in a while, something very difficult may come our way and when it does, it's a challenge to rise to that opportunity and in the process we may learn some stark life lessons or get exposed to some blunt realities of life.

Learning **the art of patience or endurance** for instance. We have been told that the road to **peace** is not a sprint but is more like a marathon. It takes a lot of patience to tread the road. It's always difficult to stand up for your opinion or defend your convictions. However, that's an opportunity given to us. To learn, to suffer and to stand up to all these opportunities given to us, tests our mettle. People avail themselves of those opportunities and leave behind legacies of learning are the ones that **we admire**. Winners make something out of life but those who fail get another opportunity. We always get another opportunity since life is composed of renewed chances.

That's the wonderful richness of life.

You should open all your senses to this wonderful richness that is given to us. There is no end to it and that is what life is all about; to enjoy what is given to us. Then we can also **open our hearts**, for the opportunities, **to help others**, to **make others happy** because nothing makes us happier than when **all of us are happy**. When we open our hearts to the opportunities, the opportunities invite us to do something,

What we can do is whatever life offers to us in that present moment, mostly it's the opportunity to enjoy but sometimes it's something more difficult. Whatever it is, if we take this opportunity and go with it, we and the people who associate with us acquire the verity of being creative.

You must open your heart to all kinds of love. You must never avoid your feelings. You must fully acknowledge your feelings

61

and let them pass. You need to give permission to yourself to experience and express your feelings authentically. **Your true authentic self is already made up of unconditional love.**

- From my previous book (: Happy Transformation :)

H.A.P.P.Y.
T.R.A.N.S.F.O.**R**.M.A.T.I.O.N.

(: Reason :)

"Reasons are the pillars of the mind."-
Edward Counsel

We are the creatures who seek the reason for
almost everything happening with us,
around us as well as things happening all
around the world. We are driven by a
particular reason for everything we do.
Reason is a tool to understand and integrate
your perceptions into concepts. We go on to
establish more clarity by evaluating and
manipulating those ideas and facts.

Your reason for wanting to do anything is
your constant reminder that keeps you
grounded, energized and focused. We are, at
some point of our lifetime, driven by our
emotional, mental, physical and spiritual
reactions to everything that happens to us.
We are willing to accept and embrace the
change when we understand how much
sense the reason makes to us.

For example, let's look once again to the real story of Sam Botta mentioned in the third chapter of my previous book Happy Transformation. He had a terrible car accident. He was a top radio voiceover artist and he literally lost the ability to speak due to a head-on car collision. He had a reason to bounce back.

Explanation behind the reason is an important key for understanding why particular things happen. Clarity comes by explanation which gives satisfaction. Research has suggested that taking time to explain flourishes personal and professional relationships and thereby promotes health and well-being.

Reason is about how to think properly and requires people to be open to change their mind. It tries to avoid bias and find the truth whether we like the truth or not. One of the core ideas of the reasoning tradition is that the truth is not obvious. Reason is about how to treat ideas, agreements, and disagreements with an assessment of unbiased maturity. It helps in learning better ideas. We must be aware that mistakes are meant to happen even when we're really sure but still there might be a possibility of mistake. Mistakes make things go wrong in our life, might hurt people and our attempts to achieve might not work out the way we desired.

Reason is the catalyst to form judgments by the process of logic. It needs the power of the mind to think, observe, analyze and understand to take further action. We need to use our own judgment to spot errors and try to do something about them. Ignoring our inherent judgment in our approach to knowledge is taking away a possible source of error correction.

Reason is used in all fields of human endeavor to make progress. For example, the scientific method is a kind of reason. The scientific method is a meta-tradition that doesn't tell us what to think directly, instead it tells us about how to seek the truth.

For example, The Harvard study of adult development mentioned in the second chapter of my previous book Happy Transformation - "To get the clearest picture of these lives, we don't just send them questionnaires. We interview them in their living rooms. We get their medical records from their doctors. We draw their blood, scan their brains and talk to their children. We videotape them talking to their wives about their deepest concerns. We've learned three big lessons about relationships." - Robert Waldinger.

Therefore, reason is an intellectual development initiated in several ways including study, observation, analysis, contemplation and by taking key lessons from experiences.

"Everything happens for a reason, but they all lessons."- Lil Boosie

H.A.P.P.Y.
T.R.A.N.S.F.O.R.M.A.T.I.O.N.

(: Motivation :)

"Believe you can and you're halfway there."- Theodore Roosevelt

Motivation improves our lives by having valuable insights from human nature. Motivation helps us in understanding why we have psychological desires, experience of emotions, set goals to strive for achievement and success. Motivation is a pathway to change our way of feeling, thinking, understanding, implementing, and behaving in a certain way to get the desired results. It allows us to gain insights about personal growth, performance and well-being. It helps us to understand why particular types of motivation are more beneficial than others. We get key learnings which are valuable to understand what aspects of it can or cannot change.

Motivation is an essential driving tool that helps in adapting as per changing circumstances. For example, the current pandemic situation of COVID-19 is teaching us a lot of lessons on how to adapt. We all need to take corrective actions as per fluctuating circumstances. Therefore, motivation is needed to direct us with guidelines for how we must live our lives in response to changes in our environment.

Motivation is crucial in maintaining our well-being and our ability to function productively. Motivation is linked to our physiology. Our psychological state gets affected with the change in motivation.

High quality and enhanced motivation allows us to thrive. Some studies show that when we feel helpless in exerting control for example, we tend to give up quickly when challenged (Peterson, Maier, & Seligman, 1993). Others have proven that when we find ourselves coerced, we lose access to our inner motivational resources (Deci, 1995).

The motivation that underlies addictive behaviors shares the neurological underpinning associated with the dopamine centric rewards system and tricky inner working of the pleasure cycle.

We must be motivated enough to control or overcome behaviours like addiction of gambling or excessive gadgets usage and unnecessary risk taking. It is challenging and difficult to change behaviour in case of unhealthy fluctuations in motivation.

We must find ways to increase our motivation in the face of constantly changing opportunities and threats. Motivation is a vital resource that helps in developing competencies by allowing us to change behaviour. Motivation helps in applying our potential in everyday life to set goals - planning and execution, grow interests, be creative and boost engagement. This increased motivation can be seen in those people who have better job satisfaction, greater social engagements and thereby having flourishing relationships.

"There are no limits to what you can accomplish, except the limits you place on your own thinking."- Brian Tracy

H.A.P.P.Y.
T.R.A.N.S.F.O.R.M.A.T.I.O.N.

(: Adequate Sleep :)

"Sleep is like the golden chain that binds our health and body together."
- Thomas Dekker

Sleep plays a vital role in good health and well-being throughout your life. Getting enough quality sleep at the right times can help protect your mental health, physical health, quality of life, and safety.

Research suggests that individuals with sleep abnormalities are also at greater risk of serious adverse health, economic consequences and most importantly increased all-cause mortality.

You must embrace the necessity of adequate sleep regularly. Adequate sleep is an important part of your daily routine. It helps in maintaining optimal health and well-being. Sleep helps your brain work properly. While you're sleeping, your brain is preparing for the next day. It's forming new pathways to help you learn and remember information.

Studies show that a good night's sleep improves learning. Whether you're learning math, how to play the piano, how to perfect your golf swing, or how to drive a car, sleep helps enhance your learning and problem-solving skills. Sleep also helps you pay attention, make decisions, and be creative.

Studies also show that sleep deficiency alters activity in some parts of the brain. If you're sleep deficient, you may have trouble making decisions, solving problems, controlling your emotions and behavior, and coping with change. Sleep deficiency also has been linked to depression, suicide, and risk-taking behavior.

Several research studies support the associations among sleep, immune function and inflammation. Research suggests better sleep quality helps the body fight off infection. Therefore, a stronger immune system and enabling the body to repair, regenerate and recover, regulate comes from a discipled regimen of sleep. Study shows there is a link between adequate sleep and reducing inflammation in the body. It helps in promoting good mental health by preventing mental illness like depression and anxiety. Also, studies suggest emotional empathy gets better with adequate amounts of sleep.

Research shows that inadequate sleep raises concerns for health problems including blood pressure, type2 diabetes, obesity which further raises the risk for heart diseases, heart attack, and stroke. Sleep apnea can be caused by certain health problems, such as obesity and heart failure. Insomnia is also linked to high blood pressure and cardiac malfunction.

The way you feel while you're awake depends in part on what happens while you're sleeping. With enough sleep each night, you may find that you're happier and more productive during the day. You must focus on building healthy habits including adequate sleep, water intake, healthy food choices and motivate yourself to be physically active to avoid the concerns over health problems and promote overall better health and well-being. Being physically active with adequate sleep promotes better athletic performances. Sleep patterns affect the hormones responsible for appetite. So, adequate sleep helps in better calorie regulation.

Adequate sleep is needed for proper cognitive and behavioral functions otherwise there is a chance of serious repercussions. There were several studies where researchers had concluded that sleep has links to several brain functions including concentration, productivity and cognition. Some studies have shown that sleep deprivation leaves people vulnerable to attention lapses, reduced cognition, delayed reactions, and mood shifts. People may not be aware of a few deficiencies like tolerance to chronic sleep deprivation in which less sleep feels normal to them. They are not aware that their brains and bodies struggle due to lack of sleep. Studies show that sleep loss has also a detrimental effect on the ability to process emotional information of an individual.

Cerebrospinal fluid(CSF) clears waste from the brain. In what's called the glymphatic system, waste products from the interstitial fluid surrounding brain cells move into the CSF and away from the brain, according to the Society for Neuroscience. Studies suggest this waste clearance process mostly happens during sleep.

In a 2013 science paper, researchers reported that when mice were asleep, their interstitial spaces expanded by 60%, and the brain's glymphatic system cleared beta-amyloid (the protein that makes up Alzheimer's disease's hallmark plaques) faster than when the rodents were awake.

Clearing potentially neurotoxic waste from the brain or "taking out the trash" through the glymphatic system could be one reason that sleep is so important, the authors suggested in their paper.

H.A.P.P.Y.
T.R.A.N.S.F.O.R.M.A.**T**.I.O.N.

(: Train your Brain :)

"Your brain is the organ of your personality, character, and intelligence and is heavily involved in making you who you are."
- Daniel G. Amen

The brain is the most complex part of the human body that is the seat of intelligence, is a interpretation of the senses, initiator of body movement, and controller of behavior. The brain is the source of all the qualities that define our humanity.

You must know a few facts about your brain and then be aware of how to train your brain. It may help you understand how the healthy brain works, how to keep it healthy, and what happens when the brain is diseased or dysfunctional.

The human brain is the command centre for the human nervous system. All sensations, feelings, thoughts, memories, movements are the result of signals that pass through neurons. The brain receives signals from the body's sensory organs and outputs information to the muscles with the help of the nervous system.

Cerebrum is the largest part of the human brain. Cerebrum is divided into two hemispheres each consists of four lobes:

1- Frontal lobe is responsible for cognitive functions like logic, abstract thought, planning, problem solving, judgment, and control of voluntary movements. It is associated with higher level motor functions including self-control which basically are the things particularly that makes us human.

2- Parietal lobe integrates inputs from different senses - sensations, handwriting, body position, spatial orientation and navigation.

3- Temporal lobe creates memories, emotions, and involves hearing.

4- Occipital lobe contains a visual processing system.

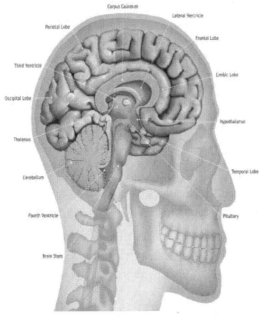

Human Brain Anatomy(Image Credit: Mark Garlick/Getty Images)

Brainstem functions include relaying information between brain and body, supplying most of the cranial nerves to the face and head and performing critical functions in controlling the heart, respiration and levels of consciousness - involved in controlling wake and sleep cycles.

The thalamus relays sensory and motor signals to the cortex except olfaction - sense of smell.

The cerebellum has important functions in motor control. It coordinates movement and balance and may also have some cognitive functions. Sports like table tennis or playing piano activates cerebellum.

The brain also has four interconnected cavities, called ventricles, which produce what's called cerebrospinal fluid (CSF). This fluid circulates around the brain and spinal cord, cushioning it from injury, and is eventually absorbed into the bloodstream.

In addition to cushioning the central nervous system, CSF clears waste from the brain. Studies suggest this waste clearance process mostly happens during sleep.

The human brain is divided into two hemispheres:

1- The left brain controls the muscles on the right side of the body.
2- The right brain controls the muscles on the left side of the body

For example, a stroke in the right hemisphere of the brain can leave the left arm and leg paralyzed.
One hemisphere may be slightly dominant due to left-handedness or right handedness.

The left brain involves in:
Language production and comprehension, mathematical calculation and fact retrieval.

The right brain involves in:
Visual and auditory processing, spatial skills and artistic ability - more instinctive or creative things.

Above functions involve both hemispheres and everyone uses both halves all the time.
For instance, the ability to form words seems to lie primarily in the left hemisphere, while the right hemisphere seems to control many abstract reasoning skills.

In order to train your brain, you need to do various activities and exercises including all your sensory perception which creates a positive health effect on all levels -

emotional, mental, physical and spiritual. All these levels affect your brain efficiency. Research suggests that using all your senses helps in strengthening your brain. Learning, implementing and teaching new skills is one of the best ways to improve the connections in your brain as well as with people. Your intention to be consistent in self-care results in better brain efficiency.

The research studies support that regularly practicing yoga, meditation and physical activities improve cognitive processes and reduce stress. Researchers have found that adequate sleep and social connections also help in alleviating symptoms of stress, anxiety and depression and boost your mood. These are indispensable medicines to improve cognitive processes and overall subjective well-being.

So basically you could hardwire your neural pathways to think positive.

How specifically to think positively?

The three techniques mentioned in chapter 3 of my previous book Happy Transformation show how you can use your body and mind to create changes. How to use your physiology to make small changes in your unconscious mind to program the neural pathways to happiness.

So, you can actually program unconsciously by certain activities and can see if you can hardwire yourself to happiness so that you can always be positive.

"Progress is impossible without change, and those who cannot change their minds cannot change anything."
      - George Bernard Shaw

H.A.P.P.Y.
T.R.A.N.S.F.O.R.M.A.T.I.O.N.

(: Intuition :)

"The more you trust your intuition, the more empowered you become, the stronger you become, and the happier you become."
- Gisele Bündchen

Have you ever felt like you were being watched, and on turning around, found someone staring at you?

Have you ever thought about someone you had not been in contact with for a while and suddenly that person had given you a call on that same day?

Does your little voice whisper to you that something is right or wrong? Or that a shiver has run down your back warning you about something?

All these are examples of intuition. The truth is that people rely on intuition to help them make decisions in a number of situations every day.

Research reveals that intuition is the most important kind of intelligence. Intuition is an automatic feeling of immediate knowledge, understanding and awareness. It appears suddenly that neither comes from reasoning or perception. It is a process that allows one to know something without conscious analytical thought.

Intuitively, our brains work based on collective intelligence and have the ability to discern which information is essential and which is not. It usually comes with a sense of certainty. We cannot explain where it came from but it has the only purpose to provide you with information you need at that particular moment.

Your intuition helps you identify your purpose in life. Since your intuition is attuned to your subconscious, it can guide you to the right direction and help you identify dreams that are aligned with your core values and your true sense of purpose.

According to research, intuition helps us to make better decisions. Our decisions are more subjective in nature. It is influenced by a combination of tacit knowledge, judgments, heuristics and intuition. Intuition is a powerful, scientifically backed skill which gives us confidence in decisions we make in our personal and professional life.

Intuitive thinking arises from the subconscious mind having a large amount of information. Your subconscious mind processes everything you experience and stores all the insights gained from these experiences. This means that your intuition started developing from the day you were born and keeps developing and expanding each day.

When you make decisions by intuition, your subconscious draws information from all your experiences and insights since birth; our long term memory and any know-how acquired through associated learning, trying to identify patterns or anomalies. Then use it to provide us with cues about the current situation. Since these cues seem to come from the gut, it is not surprising that some scientists refer to the gut as a second brain.

Therefore, you can also say that intuition depends on data, only that you don't analyze the data consciously. Since your subconscious is faster and has a wider pool of information to draw from, it is sometimes more reliable than rational decision making.

Intuitive decision making is a decision making approach that is less structured and more fluid compared to other approaches like rationalistic decision making. Intuition does not follow any series of steps. Instead of itemizing parts of the problem, it considers the whole picture.

Secondly, intuition does not rely on the analytical, conscious part of the mind. This is why most people have a hard time explaining intuitive decisions or perceptions. Finally, intuitive decision making relies more on emotions and feelings instead of facts and figures. How does this happen?

People who rely on their intuition are more open to new ideas. The rational mind relies on logical patterns which can sometimes be limiting. Intuition, on the other hand, sees things that your rational mind is oblivious to, allowing you to recognize new opportunities.

The survey conducted on top executives found that the majority of top leaders turn to their experience and feelings when making important decisions. Another study found that 81% of CEOs who exhibited high levels of intuition doubled their business within five years.

Scientists and researchers have realized the importance of intuition, which is why data scientists and machine learning experts have started combining data science and intuition for more robust results. The scientists are not alone. Even the military has realized the importance of intuition, which is why the U.S. Navy invested $3.85 million to help Marines and sailors hone their intuition.

Intuition is especially important in situations where a decision needs to be made instantly, without time to consider the different aspects of the situation. One of the greatest advantages of intuition is that it allows you to make decisions in complex and unfamiliar situations quickly and effectively. Think about first responders responding to an emergency, or a soldier in the heat of battle. In both situations, there is no luxury of time. Taking a few seconds to think things through is literally a matter of life and death.

Even going back in history, we find that intuition has always been an important skill.

Most of the world's greatest inventions and discoveries, from the discovery of penicillin by Alexander Fleming to the detection of X-rays by Wilhelm Rontgen, all happened due to intuition. More recently, successful entrepreneurs like Steve Jobs, Bill Gates, Richard Branson and Elon Musk have credited part of their success to their intuition.

" Follow your instincts. That's where true wisdom manifests itself." - Oprah Winfrey

Intuition helps you read people. For instance, you might be talking to a client who says that he will hire your company, while his body suggests that he has no plans of working with you. Intuition can help you sense such signs, allowing you to tweak your approach in order to retain the client. Sometimes, this can be the difference between success and failure. Intuition also acts as a cautionary voice. Sometimes, you might overlook some risks even after carefully analyzing a situation rationally. Intuition can tell you when something feels off, allowing you to steer clear of situations that would have otherwise turned out badly.

Intuition gives you access to deeper intelligence and wisdom.

"I believe in intuitions and inspirations. I sometimes feel that I am right. I don't know that I am." - Albert Einstein

H.A.P.P.Y.
T.R.A.N.S.F.O.R.M.A.T.I.O.N.

(: Open to noble causes :)

"Since you get more joy out of giving joy to others, you should put a good deal of thought into the happiness that you are able to give."-Eleanor Roosevelt

The inspiring real story of a mom and 3 year old kid from the Happy Transformation book teaches us to be a giver.

You must give back something to the world. You must be kind, helpful and benevolent to people, animals and our planet. You ought to spread happiness by giving. The more you spread happiness, the more your life becomes meaningful.

You have this free gift of giving. Giving must be your daily routine, make it a habit. You need to understand that your actions have a ripple effect around you within your family, friends and community. You can choose the way you want to bring a positive impact to the world. You need to inspire people all around the world to be selfless and benevolent. Giving inspires giving.

Of course, we can give in many ways:

1-we can give money if we've got some to spare.

2-we can give time.

3-we can give our skills.

4-we can give a helping hand.

5-we can give a moment of thoughtful attention.

We have all heard that giving makes you happy and it's better to give than to receive.

But have you actually thought why?

Well, researchers from all over the world have been studying the science and psychology of giving. They have discovered that our brains and our bodies are actually hardwired for giving. Giving creates a "warm glow", biologically, which activates regions in the brain that are associated with pleasure. It enables you to make connections with other people; to build your trust with other people; to feel the excitement and closeness to them during giving; makes you feel happy to volunteer for such experiences.

There is evidence that humans secrete chemicals in their brains during gifting. The chemicals are Serotonin which is a mood-mediating chemical or the body's transmitter of happiness, Dopamine which is a feel-good chemical, and Oxytocin which is compassion and bonding chemical. Our Oxytocin level rises while giving, releasing our love hormone and for those who have been looking for the **fountain of youth**, this is our body's natural anti-aging remedy. The biggest positive through this act however is the reduction in our Cortisol levels, which is the stress enhancing hormone.

The people who donate for various charitable causes, bear semblances of happiness inside them. When you look at the functional MRIs of these people, scientists have found that giving stimulates the *Mesolimbic* pathway, which is the reward center in the brain. The brain releases Endorphins and creates what is known as the "**helper's high**" and like other highs, this one is addictive too. So you must go ahead and reach out to someone in need. You can decide what charities you'd like to do.

You must identify opportunities to give back to your community and society at large. This gives you a boost to your emotional, mental, physical, and spiritual health taking social factors into account.

We have been taking so many things from this planet and we have been so lucky to get them. However, not everyone is so lucky. Therefore, people like us should be kind enough to give back certain things to people who need them more than we do.

Giving reduces anxiety and stress and makes us happy.

Donate, volunteer, help a neighbor, be kind to a stranger.

This is how we're going to go from anxiety and depression to happiness.

Together, we can all start small, and we can make the world a better world, a happier world.

"While it may seem small, the ripple effects of small things is extraordinary."
- Matt Bevin

- From my previous book (: Happy Transformation :)

H.A.P.P.Y.
T.R.A.N.S.F.O.R.M.A.T.I.O.N.

(: Needs :)

"We are all capable of achieving whatever we want and need." - Paulo Coelho

What are your needs?
What do you want?
Is your want valid?

What motivates human behaviour?

Human actions are motivated in order to achieve certain needs.

What makes you happy?

Your needs are responsible for your own deeds. You are in a happy state when your needs are fulfilled. The satisfaction towards your life is an important factor. A need is something that is necessary and required for a safe, stable and healthy life. The needs are powerful enough to influence human behavior.

The physiological needs that are vital to survive are air, water, food, land, shelter - protection from environmental dangers. It also includes temperature regulation - homeostasis, clothing and reproduction - essential to the survival and propagation of the human species.

A want is a desire. Economic demand is a potential need or want backed by purchasing power.

There is a psychological need that gives purpose to humans that requires them to take action that gives direction to their particular behaviour towards achieving that particular goal. It may vary among different cultures or different parts of the same society.

In addition, there are human needs of safety and security, love and friendship, esteem and feeling of accomplishments. These needs are deficiency needs which arise due to deprivation. Therefore, these needs are needed to be satisfied to avoid unpleasant feelings or consequences.

Examples of actions motivated by the security and safety needs include:- earning, saving and investing money through job or business - financial security, health care and insurance, better and safer neighborhoods.

There is also a need of human societal nature to socialize to a family unit or a group. Social needs are beneficial to avoid or overcome loneliness and depression, suicidal tendencies, stress and anxiety. (to know more, kindly refer Happy Transformation book no.1 of the series)

Therefore, it is important for people to feel connected to others - family, friends and community for love, peace, joy, acceptance and a sense of belonging. Thus, keeping themselves healthy on levels - emotional, mental, physical, spiritual for a blissful life.

At some point in their life, people feel that they are contributing to the world, their work must be recognized and appreciated. They need to accomplish something and have a sense of fulfillment. Their accomplished efforts lead to better self-esteem and worthy enough to be recognized and respected.

People engaging themselves in their hobbies, participating in sports teams or any professional activities, community services, academic accomplishments gives satisfaction and fulfilling their esteem needs. This boosts their confidence and ability to grow better as a person.

People are self-aware and keep on bettering their talents and capabilities for contribution. People have an inborn desire to be self - actualized, that is, to be all they can be. It's a process of growing and developing as a person in order to achieve individual potential. This is considered a growth need - desire to grow as a person.

```
********************************
```
Abraham Maslow
```
********************************
```

Humans are considered as needy creatures. They undergo the process of learning and working to meet their needs and have a suffering experience to do so. These needs are physical, moral, emotional, and intellectual needs.

According to Karl Marx, human development is characterized by the fact that in the process of meeting their needs, humans develop new needs, implying that at least to some extent they make and remake their own nature.

"Every person has an objective interest in avoiding serious harm that prevents that person from endeavoring to attain his vision of what is good, regardless of what exactly that may be. That endeavour requires a capacity to participate in the societal setting in which the individual lives. More specifically, every person needs to possess both physical health and personal autonomy. The latter involves the capacity to make informed choices about what should be done and how to implement it. This requires mental health, cognitive skills, and opportunities to participate in society's activities and collective decision-making."

- Gough and Doyal

You do understand the value of a particular need to be achieved in your life. At the same time you also have the satisfaction which you already have.

"Prioritize your needs and discipline your wants." - Filibus Promise

Conclusion

"Energy"

"Energy can neither be created nor destroyed; rather, it can only be transformed or transferred from one form to another."

- The Law of Conservation of Energy

H.A.P.P.Y. T.R.A.N.S.F.O.R.M.A.T.I.O.N. is a journey to transform you and amplify your happiness so that you inspire, illuminate, touch and enlighten others through your presence. In the process of transforming yourself, you're also transferring the positive energy of happiness all around. Thereby creating positive ripple effects.

You might have realized that in all the above topics - H to N are somehow interconnected, interrelated, synchronistic and coherent.

You must understand the concept and context which is covered in this book and take action to move one step ahead. Your next step is to start practicing the concepts that have been mentioned. It's your journey as a beginner to intermediate and then maintain at the advanced level. These all are covered in the next books in the series.

In the introduction, there is a question to be answered.

The 5th stage is: Conscious Unconscious competence

"I can explain how I do it with ease to others".

This stage shows the importance of retention power.

Research shows that people who learn, implement and teach to others have high retention of a particular knowledge.

So, it's time for you to unleash the power of now. Now you have the knowledge so act now, be an action taker, start giving time to yourself since self-education is the best investment of time, money and effort. The golden triangle principle - learn, do and teach; so, first give time to yourself for self education then implement those and understand the nuances and then give time to others, teach them who wants to spread awareness and happiness. Let's all have a H.A.P.P.Y. T.R.A.N.S.F.O.R.M.A.T.I.O.N. life. Be the cause to inspire, illuminate, touch, and enlighten me through your presence and create a positive ripple effect on others' lives.

Intention of writing this book is to bring a positive impact to the reader's life.

This book emphasizes on readers' happiness. How we imagine our happiness differs from one person to the other but it's already a lot that we all have in common, the foremost is that we want to be happy.

Even if it brings about positive impact on any reader, it does make a difference!

It's worth taking action for writing a book that brings about positive impact. I believe that this book will do the same.

Always be grateful for what you have and what you can give!

The realization that your life can be helpful and can inspire other people, brings about an unadulterated feeling of liberty and bliss.

What's your Happy Transformation score ?
Why do you need to calculate a Happy Transformation score?

How to calculate a Happy Transformation score?

You will know in the upcoming books of the series.

Please do share your reviews and if you find this book valuable and useful enough to share with others about H.A.P.P.Y. T.R.A.N.S.F.O.R.M.A.T.I.O.N. awareness to reach the natural default set of **Happy Transformation**.

Always be grateful for what you have and what you can give.

It's not happiness that makes us grateful. It's gratefulness that makes us happy.

"Show Gratitude"

As

"Positive Intentions Bring Positive Results"

Upcoming books

HAPPY TRANSFORMATION

**Activities book | Journal | Lessons
Learnt | Inspiring Facts**

Already published book

The Positive Ripple Effect

HAPPY TRANSFORMATION

Methods to Overcome Depression, Stress & Anxiety for Better Brain Health, and to Cherish Happy Relationships

Link of my 1st book of the series:

Buy Now!

For Overseas :

https://www.amazon.com/Happy-Transformation-Overcome-Depression-Relationships-ebook/dp/B0929JBCJ1/ref=sr_1_1?dchild=1&keywords=happy+transformation&qid=1623730977&sr=8-1

For India :

https://www.amazon.in/Happy-Transformation-Overcome-Depression-Relationships-

ebook/dp/B0929JBCJ1/ref=sr_1_1?crid=3S
E60QY1UYAZL&dchild=1&keywords=happy
+transformation&qid=1623731270&sprefix=
happy+tra%2Caps%2C370&sr=8-1

Share or embed a free Kindle book preview :

https://read.amazon.in/kp/embed?asin=B0
929JBCJ1&preview=newtab&linkCode=kpe
&ref_=cm_sw_r_kb_dp_4X3JTXG573HW
47Y5RZRP

The reviews of this book :

CreativeKarma
5.0 out of 5 stars **I am experiencing the happiness...now!**

Happy Transformation is such a wonderful book!

Usually, to get best out of the book, you need to follow the advice given by the author. I found this book quite different. While reading the book itself I could feel a 'happy transformation' happening within me.

I found some of the concepts mentioned in the book, namely 'Give 360' and 'ripple effect', quite powerful

The authors speaks about the things that resonate with me so well – Giving and gratitude. I believe, these are the basic ingredients of happiness. Practice them and experience happy transformation in your life

Rajib Dutta
5.0 out of 5 stars **Happiness is like a that rainfall in a dry desert.**

Happiness is like the oxygen in this present scenario of covid. So the author has done a profound work to radiate happiness to the mind of the readers like a sweet pill.

I recommend this book to everybody.

Jenny
5.0 out of 5 stars **Stress free life**

Stress being part of everyone's life needs to be relieved to live a happy and healthy life..this book is perfect to deal with such life issues and keep you .motivated..thanks to author for sharing these wonderful thoughts..

B J RAO

5.0 out of 5 stars **Giving is living with happiness.As you sow,so you reap.**

Happy Transformation is the effort made by the author for spreading happiness.
The name of the book well chosen, which will give the readers some thought of trying to live with happiness.
It is about how giving,helping others,relationship,responsibility turn anxiety,depression into happiness.This is well expressed by author by his thoughts and words.

Sneha Rajput

5.0 out of 5 stars **Read the book for happiness**

Giving is more than accepting. The basic way for transformation is to begin serving. Meditation releasing stress is explained by the author in simple language. I enjoyed reading the book to remain happy.

Apurva

5.0 out of 5 stars **Amazing Transformational book**

Excellent Read, Transformations should happen from within and the methodologies explained in this book help us achieve these transformations. Awesome!!!

Satadal

5.0 out of 5 stars☐**An appropriate book of the times.**

This is a book on happiness and how to attain and retain it.

Very appropriate at this juncture of life and relevant for all.

Dr K.R.S

5.0 out of 5 stars☐**A compelling book to create all round happiness and prosperity**

As claimed by the author, this is a book intended to inspire people to understand the value of giving and creating happiness thereby.

Among the noteworthy points are the power of the positive ripple effect, gratitude that is precursor to happiness and the master key to happiness lying within. And the key takeaways include: '75 per cent of your state is your inside environment and 25 per cent, the outside environment' and the inside environment is responsible for 80 per cent of one's circumstances, whereas the remaining 20 per cent is created by the outside environment.

In short, what is suggested is that we're all having an inside-out paradigm of life. A thought provoking book that can transform the lives of discerning readers. Kudos to the author.

GSK
5.0 out of 5 stars☐**Provides a practical approach to lead a happy life!**

"Happy Transformation" is a simple yet powerful book filled with practical and effective techniques to not just lead a happy life... it also spreads happiness to those around us. I resonate totally with the concept of giving back to the community and planet earth. Written in a simple language, the content when applied can transform one's life.

Lalit Hundalani

4.0 out of 5 stars **Must read and very engaging**

The book is very appropriate for current scenario where mental health is a big concern. Author has shared various techniques to curtail negative emotions.Being a Transformation coach myself,really appreciate and can truly resonate with the author' intent of helping people.

Ratna Rao

4.0 out of 5 stars **A book to possess**

Relationships bring us joy and they bring heartache. The author has put forth many tried and tested methods of building stronger relationships. If you seek a happy life, buy and read this wonderful book.

Bikash Paul Choudhury
5.0 out of 5 stars **A well researched book**

The author explained the importance of
giving and outlined and elaborated the
connection of giving with happiness in the
realm of relationship, intention, actions and
gratitude. It's a very good book - a keepsake
as appeared to me.

Acknowledgments

I am grateful to all the people who have inspired me to write this book.

I cannot thank my parents, siblings, teachers, mentors (especially Mr. Som Bathla), friends, colleagues and well wishers enough.

My deepest gratitude to every person who has come into my life to inspire, illuminate, touch, and enlighten me through their presence.

I wish to acknowledge and express my gratitude to the people who are associated with the links given at the end of this book for contributions to my research journey and to the creation of this book.

I wish to express my gratitude to the editor and proofreader of this book- Satadal Lahiri. And book cover designed by Ravendesigns.

Last but by no means the least I shall always remain grateful to the readers of this book. They mean a lot to me.

About The Author

B. R. "Amritaanshu" Saroj

Numero-Vastu Expert

Holistic Health Mentor

Author | Health Podcaster

Earth Collaborator

"Prevention is better than cure."

B.R. Amritaanshu Saroj is serving as a Holistic Health Mentor @ awareonc - social initiative: Cancer awareness among the younger generation.

His work as a Holistic Health Mentor for awareonc is to consult for analyzing and understanding the root causes of cancer at the primordial and primary levels of prevention and then providing the various remedies and solutions by taking a holistic approach. A holistic approach helps people to work on their potential to be a better version of themselves.

Preventive measures can be applied at any stage along the natural history of the disease with the goal of preventing further progression of the condition.

His work is at the level of primordial prevention and primary prevention.

Primordial prevention

Primordial prevention consists of actions to minimize future hazards to health and hence inhibits the establishment of factors that are known to increase the risk of disease. It addresses broad health determinants rather than preventing personal exposure to risk factors, which is the goal of primary prevention.

Primary prevention

Primary prevention seeks to prevent the onset of specific diseases via risk reduction by altering behaviors or exposures that can lead to disease or by enhancing resistance to the effects of exposure to a disease agent.

Awareonc Primary Prevention:

1. Promoting cancer awareness at the family level for healthy eating and correcting lifestyle-associated risk factors.

2. Educating health to the younger generation.

3. Banning tobacco products.

4. Limiting processed food including the red meat intake.

5. Training Health Ambassadors for community teaching.

Courtesy:@

Awareonc Founder & Director

B. R. Achyut, Ph.D.

Cancer Scientist & Educator

Amritaanshu is working as a Numero-Vastu Expert and helping people to work on their potential through a combination of Numerology and Vastu along with few other techniques and bringing positive changes in their lives.

He believes that his moral responsibility as an Author is to spread awareness, motivate, etc. His **intention** is to bring a **positive impact** to the reader's life, thereby creating a **positive ripple effect**.

He has planned to start his solo podcast as well as interview podcast as a Health Podcaster to spread awareness, motivate, etc. to his podcast listeners. His intention is to create a **Health Transformation** that makes his listeners - _Happy as well as Cherish all types of Quality Relationships for a Grateful Abundance Life_.

His Dream Project

To serve as an **Earth Collaborator ... to add value...on a mission...vision...**framework he will be sharing soon on his website.

He is grateful to you for taking out the time to read above.

Cheers!

To your blissful life.

References

(: Happy Transformation :) Book no.1 of the series.

(: Higher levels of Consciousness :)

https://medium.com/mind-cafe/how-to-achieve-a-higher-level-of-consciousness-and-go-beyond-the-mind-90537807f32a

(: Happy Transformation :) Book no.1 of the series.

(: Awareness :)

https://positivepsychology.com/self-awareness-matters-how-you-can-be-more-self-aware/

https://www.verywellmind.com/what-is-self-awareness-2795023

https://deepakchopra.medium.com/the-importance-of-being-aware-3308e2918020

https://believeperform.com/the-importance-of-awareness/

https://www.handinhandqc.org/post/2017/03/08/the-importance-of-awareness#:~:text=Awareness%20of%20people's%20differences%20from,open%20minded%20and%20less%20judgmental.&text=Awareness%20can%20also%20lead%20to,who%20are%20different%20than%20yourself.

(: Purpose :)

https://pubmed.ncbi.nlm.nih.gov/26630073/

https://jamanetwork.com/journals/jamapsychiatry/fullarticle/2648692

https://www.trackinghappiness.com/important-to-have-purpose-in-life/

https://katesiner.com/finding-purpose-important

https://stunningmotivation.com/purpose-is-important/

https://www.beyondblue.org.au/docs/default-source/senseability/sense-of-purpose-handout.pdf?sfvrsn=2#:~:text=It%20is%20important%20to%20know,achieve%20what%20you%20strived%20for.

(: Happy Transformation :) Book no.1 of the series.

(: Personal Development :)

https://harappa.education/harappa-diaries/personal-or-self-development

https://www.liveyourtruestory.com/core-benefits-personal-development-performance/

https://stunningmotivation.com/personal-development-important/

(: You :)

https://www.thehopeline.com/5-amazing-reasons-why-you-matter/

https://www.meaningfullife.com/50-reasons-why-your-life-matters/

https://www.helenedwardswrites.com/10-reasons-why-you-matter/

https://www.authentic.com.au/blog/speaking/how-to-share-your-message-with-the-world/

(: Happy Transformation :) Book no.1 of the series.

(:Technical development:)

https://www.opencolleges.edu.au/blog/201
9/04/30/the-importance-of-developing-
your-technical-skills-right-
now/#:~:text=Technology%20is%20gradual
ly%20infiltrating%20every,decisions%20fas
ter%2C%20and%20much%20more.

https://hardeebusiness.com/resources/tech
nologys-role-in-economic-development

https://www.immerse.education/articles/w
hy-are-tech-skills-so-important-to-todays-
students/

(: Resilience :)

https://www.counselling-
directory.org.uk/memberarticles/the-
importance-of-building-
resilience#:~:text=Resilience%20is%20imp
ortant%20for%20several,mental%20health
%20difficulties%20and%20issues.

https://www.verywellmind.com/what-is-
resilience-2795059

https://positivepsychology.com/what-is-resilience/

https://www.mindtools.com/pages/article/resilience.htm

https://www.lifehack.org/715558/what-is-resilience-and-how-to-be-resilient

(: Action :)

(: Happy Transformation :) Book no.1 of the series.

http://www.ilanelanzen.com/personaldevelopment/11-reasons-taking-action-is-crucial/#:~:text=Taking%20action%20helps%20you%20overcome%20your%20fears.&text=And%2C%20as%20you%20expand%20your,the%20life%20of%20your%20dreams.

https://seeken.org/important-take-action/

(: Network & Ecosystem :)

(: Happy Transformation :) Book no.1 of the series.

(: Self-conditioning :)

https://www.psychologistworld.com/memory/conditioning-intro

https://www.verywellmind.com/what-is-self-concept-2795865

https://positivepsychology.com/self-concept/

(: Happy Transformation :) Book no.1 of the series.

(:Focus :)

https://vancruzer.com/focus-is-important-in-your-life/

https://www.guidedmind.com/blog/6-benefits-of-being-more-focused

https://www.huffpost.com/entry/focus-is-the-gateway-to-b_b_4206552

(: Opportunity :)

(: Happy Transformation :) Book no.1 of the series.

https://www.youtube.com/watch?v=UtBsl3joYRQ&t=1s

(: Reason :)

https://www.psychologytoday.com/us/blog/happiness-in-world/201011/why-we-need-know-why

http://www.importanceofphilosophy.com/Epistemology_Reason.html

https://fallibleideas.com/reason

https://lawfulrebel.com/reason-guide-knowledge/

(: Happy Transformation :) Book no.1 of the series.

(: Motivation :)

https://positivepsychology.com/benefits-motivation/

https://managementstudyguide.com/importance_of_motivation.htm

https://stunningmotivation.com/why-motivation-is-important/

(: Adequate Sleep :)

https://www.nhlbi.nih.gov/health-topics/sleep-deprivation-and-deficiency

https://www.ncbi.nlm.nih.gov/pmc/articles/PMC3882397/

https://www.medicalnewstoday.com/articles/

https://www.cdc.gov/bloodpressure/sleep.htm?CDC_AA_refVal=https%3A%2F%2Fwww.cdc.gov%2Ffeatures%2Fsleep-heart-health%2Findex.html

https://www.sleepfoundation.org/how-sleep-works/why-do-we-need-sleep

(: Train your Brain :)

https://www.webmd.com/brain/picture-of-the-brain

https://www.ninds.nih.gov/Disorders/Patient-Caregiver-Education/Know-Your-Brain

https://www.livescience.com/29365-human-brain.html

(: Happy Transformation :) Book no.1 of the series.

(: Intuition :)

https://www.cleverism.com/how-intuition-helps-us-make-better-decisions/#:~:text=Your%20intuition%20helps%20you%20identify,more%20open%20to%20new%20ideas.

https://positivepsychology.com/intuition/

https://www.forbes.com/sites/bonniemarcus/2015/09/01/intuiton-is-an-essential-leadership-tool/?sh=68ddb1b61c18

https://www.powerofpositivity.com/intuition-most-important-intelligence/

https://www.aconsciousrethink.com/3270/13-absurdly-awesome-traits-highly-intuitive-people/

(: Open to noble causes :)

(: Happy Transformation :) Book no.1 of the series.

(: Needs :)

https://en.wikipedia.org/wiki/Need

https://www.verywellmind.com/what-is-maslows-hierarchy-of-needs-4136760

https://en.wikipedia.org/wiki/ERG_theory

Printed in Great Britain
by Amazon

29273277R00073